The Homemade Pasta Cookbook:

365 Days of Artful and Authentic Italian Recipes | Explore Time-Honored Techniques for Crafting the Ultimate Pasta Experience

By:
Lyra Falconer

Table of Contents

Introduction

I first experienced the enchantment of handmade pasta in the midst of a lively kitchen, where the enticing aroma of sauces being cooked low and slow and the soothing sound of water being brought to a seethe were in perfect harmony with one another. It was a transforming moment, one that took me to a world where every mouthful was a blast of taste, and every meal was a celebration of life. It was a moment that I will never forget. In the next pages of this book, I would like to introduce you to the enchanted world of pasta and encourage you to explore it.

After a long and exhausting day, do you ever have the need for a big dish of spaghetti to settle your stomach? Or maybe you've found yourself standing in front of your cupboard, starring at the package of dry pasta, and pondering whether or not there's more to this simple food than meets the eye. If you've ever been disappointed by uninspiring pasta meals or wished you could make spaghetti at home that was on par with what you get in restaurants, you're not the only one. Because I've been there myself, I completely understand the desire to find the ideal pasta dish.

The wide variety of pasta shapes, sauces, and cooking methods might make it seem to be an insurmountable challenge to perfect handmade pasta. However, there is no need for alarm since this book will serve as your illuminating beacon as you navigate the maze of pasta options. If you've ever been stumped by a pasta-related question, here is the place to go for a solution, regardless of how much experience you have in the kitchen.

Therefore, why should we go on this gastronomic excursion together? The advantages are almost overflowing like a plate of freshly topped spaghetti. In the first place, you'll have the self-assurance to create pasta meals that are on par with the ones served at your favorite Italian trattoria. You will no longer have to depend entirely on pasta that you purchase from the store since you will be able to make your own, with each noodle serving as a showcase for your culinary expertise.

This book is not merely a collection of recipes; rather, it is an exploration into new culinary lands. You'll learn how to pick the ideal pasta form for each sauce, which will allow you to make dishes that are delicious and satisfying symphony of both flavor and texture. You will delve into the world of handmade sauces, from those that are opulent and decadent to those that are light and refreshing, and you will learn how to combine these sauces with your pasta so that they complement each other perfectly. And for those mornings when you're in the mood for something a little bit different from the norm, we'll delve into the world of breakfast spaghetti, which is a lovely twist on the conventional.

But why should you look to me to be your pasta guide? Despite the fact that I do not wear a chef's hat or have a long list of degrees in the culinary arts, I am a dedicated pasta aficionado who has spent years experimenting, improving, and appreciating each and every noodle. I've experienced both the failures and the successes, so that you won't have to go through either one on your own. My adventure started with the very first bite of handmade pasta, and since then, it has developed into a full-fledged obsession with everything and everything associated with pasta. In my quest to create the ideal pasta meal, I have read a vast number of cookbooks, tried food from a variety of different countries, and practiced my abilities in my own kitchen.

But most importantly, this book is the one you should read since it was written just with you in mind. It doesn't matter whether you're a busy mom searching for ideas for fast weekday dinners, a culinary explorer ready to discover new tastes, or someone hoping to dazzle visitors at a dinner party; this article has something for everyone. This book is not just a compilation of recipes; rather, it is a passport to a universe of possibilities including pasta.

In the chapters that are to come, you will discover a treasury full of recipes that will take your game of making pasta to new heights. We will investigate the whole range of possibilities presented by pasta, from decadent morning pasta meals to enticing lunch and supper concoctions, and even a variety of scrumptious desserts based on pasta. Along the process, you'll pick up some priceless secrets, methods, and insights that will enable you to become a pasta master in the comfort of your own home kitchen.

Turn the page, dear reader, and let's go on an adventure into the realm of "Pasta Cookbook Homemade" if you're ready to start on a culinary journey that will fill your house with the enticing scent of homemade pasta. Together, we will turn your kitchen into a pasta paradise, where each meal will be a masterpiece ready to be appreciated and enjoyed.

The History of Pasta:
A Culinary Odyssey

Pasta, that delectable combination made of wheat and water, has been a mainstay on dinner tables all around the globe for a very long time. It is an intriguing culinary riddle that has left food aficionados enthralled and historians enchanted. Its roots are lost in the mists of time, making it a tantalizing culinary mystery. The history of pasta is a voyage across ages and countries; it is a monument to human invention and the widespread appeal of a dish that is both simple and adaptable like spaghetti.

A Storied Past: The Origins of Pasta

The history of pasta may be traced back to the ancient civilizations that flourished in the Mediterranean region, where both wheat and water were readily available. The Etruscans, who formerly lived in what is now Italy, are credited with developing the first meals that were conceptually similar to pasta more than 4,000 years ago. They used primitive ovens to produce a flat, unleavened bread that they called "lagane." This dough was known as "lagane."

The Etruscan method of producing pasta was taken by the Greeks, who then went on to perfect the skill of creating pasta and bring it back to their country. Around the 5th century BCE, the term "itriya," which refers to a specific type of pasta, had its first appearance in Greek literature. The proliferation of trade routes coincided with the rise in popularity of pasta, which in turn extended the cuisine's impact throughout the Mediterranean.

The Silk Road Connection

The voyage that pasta took along the old Silk Road is one of the most interesting episodes in its long and illustrious history. Not only did traders transport silk and spices on their journeys over the wide distance between China and the Mediterranean, but they also brought gastronomic wonders with them. It is generally accepted that the expertise required to make pasta made its way from Asia to the Mediterranean region through these trading channels.

It is often believed that the Chinese were the first people to create noodles, and their presence along the Silk Road most certainly played a significant part in the spread of this kind of pasta. The well-known Venetian traveler Marco Polo is credited with having written about his experiences with pasta when he was traveling in China in the 13th century. When he got back to Italy, he took noodles and skills for creating pasta with him, which kicked off a revolution in pasta production throughout Europe.

Pasta Arrives in Europe: A Culinary Renaissance

The Europeans enthusiastically embraced pasta as a staple food. The fact that it could be stored for an extended period of time without going bad made it an excellent option for seafarers setting off on lengthy journeys, and it didn't take long for it to find its way into the pantries of many more houses after that. The Renaissance saw the beginning of pasta's development into the many shapes and forms that are available today.

The Italians, in particular, developed an interest in pasta, which resulted in the creation of a bewildering variety of forms and sizes. Pasta shapes like as penne, farfalle, and fettuccine, amongst others, came to be recognized as regional specialties throughout time. Each shape was developed to be the ideal complement to a distinct sauce and set of components. This happy union of pasta and sauce established Italy as a culinary powerhouse, and the rest of the world couldn't help but fall in love with Italian food as a result.

Pasta first became widely available in the United States in the latter half of the 19th century and the early 20th century. This gastronomic delicacy was given to the New World by Italian immigrants, who carried with them their beloved traditions of pasta-making. Pasta was at first received with some reluctance by Americans, but it didn't take them very long to warm up to the idea of eating it entirely.

The first pasta factory in the United States opened its doors in Brooklyn, New York, in the year 1888. This facility produced fresh pasta for the local Italian population. Pasta swiftly became a well-loved staple food in homes all throughout the country as immigration continued to have a significant impact on the culinary scene of the United

States. In point of fact, the consumption of pasta in the United States has now surpassed that in Italy, establishing it as an essential component of the cuisine of the United States.

Types of Pasta and Their Culinary Roles

After delving into the intriguing background of pasta, it's time to focus on the real stars of the show: the many kinds of pasta and the myriad ways they may be used in the kitchen. The variety of pasta goes well beyond the varieties of spaghetti and macaroni that the majority of us are used to eating. It's a universe of different forms, sizes, and textures, each of which has been painstakingly constructed to perform a certain function.

Spaghetti is a kind of thin, round pasta that is ideal for twirling around a fork because of its slenderness and roundness. Spaghetti is often considered to be the most recognizable type of pasta. It is delicious when combined with a wide variety of sauces, from the traditional marinara to the velvety Alfredo.

Linguine, which is somewhat broader and flatter than spaghetti, is an excellent option for the preparation of delicate seafood dishes. Because of its flat surface, it is able to pick up each and every detail of the sauce.

Wider than spaghetti, fettuccine is often used as a canvas for sauces that are very rich or creamy. Who wants some Alfredo? Because of its wide design, a sumptuous pasta dish may be built upon it in the best possible way.

Penne: People who are acquainted with penne enjoy the distinctive ridges that it has, which adhere to sauces better than any other kind of pasta. It is a flexible pasta that may be prepared with either a simple tomato sauce or a more involved baked ziti dish.

Rigatoni is an excellent choice for rich, meaty sauces because to its huge tubes that are ridged all over. Because of its hollow core, it is able to capture the tastes, making each bite an experience in its own right.

Ziti is a kind of small and skinny tube pasta that is often used in baked pasta recipes. They work well as receptacles for tangy tomato sauces and smooth cheeses.

The form of farfalle, which resembles a butterfly or a bowtie, lends an air of playfulness to any pasta salad in which it is included. Its ridges and folds make it an excellent tool for collecting stray crumbs of ingredients and dressing.

Rotini: The corkscrew form of rotini is a popular in pasta salads because the grooves in the rotini do a good job of holding sauces and veggies. Cooking with this pasta is a blast because of its wide range of applications.

Orzo: Although orzo is sometimes mistaken for rice, it is really a tiny kind of pasta that is excellent for use in soups, salads, and other side dishes. Your dishes will benefit tremendously from the nutty undertone and lovely texture that it imparts.

Ravioli: Ravioli are like a cute little savory present that is just waiting to be opened. These pasta parcels with a filling of your choice may be loaded with anything from meat and veggies to cheese and herbs.

Tortellini are pasta parcels that have a form very similar to that of ravioli. Tortellini often include a combination of meats, cheeses, or vegetables. They provide a wonderful complement to soups and are delicious when served with sauces that are rich in taste.

Huge manicotti is tubular in shape, making them an ideal choice for filling with ricotta cheese and spinach. It is a traditional Italian dish that is soothing and is baked with sauce and mozzarella.

Orzo: As was just explained, orzo is a kind of very little pasta that has the appearance of grains of rice. It lends foods a distinct and interesting texture, and it works particularly well in soups, salads, and pilafs.

These little round pasta beads, known as acini di pepe, are excellent for adding to broths and soups because they absorb flavors and offer a delightfully different texture to the dish.

Ditalini, which literally translates to "little thimbles," are a kind of pasta that are often used in pasta e fagioli, a traditional Italian soup. Because of their little size, they are an excellent complement to substantial stews and soups.

Gluten-Free Varieties: In recent years, there has been an explosion in the number of gluten-free pasta alternatives that are manufactured from alternative flours such as rice, maize, and quinoa. Because of the variety of alternatives available, anybody, regardless of their dietary preferences, will be able to enjoy a wonderful pasta dish.

The tale of pasta is a fascinating one that takes place over the course of millennia and continents, and it is one that is still developing as a result of new culinary innovations. Pasta, in all of its many forms and sizes, has firmly established itself as a popular staple food all across the world. Its path is a monument to human ingenuity and adaptation, starting with the modest origins of lagane in ancient Etruria and ending in the busy pasta mills of New York City.

You are now ready to go off on your very own culinary journey, armed with a more in-depth grasp of the long and illustrious history of pasta as well as the variety of sorts of pasta at your disposal. Remember that pasta is not simply a meal; it's a canvas for your imagination and a vehicle for the culinary fantasies you've been harboring. This is important to keep in mind whether you're preparing a basin of comfortable spaghetti or experimenting with unusual forms of pasta. Now is the time to roll up your sleeves, put some water on to seethe, and get started on the process of creating pasta. Have a nice meal!

Essential Pasta-Making Equipment: Your Culinary Arsenal

Let's take a quick look at the basic tools that will turn your kitchen into a pasta paradise before we get into the ins and outs of the art of creating pasta. In the same way that a painter depends on high-quality brushes and canvas for their work, a pasta aficionado must have the appropriate instruments in order to make flawless pasta.

The Pasta Machine: Your Trusty Companion

The pasta machine is vital to any undertaking that involves the production of pasta. This useful tool is essential for rolling out pasta dough until it is absolutely thin and consistent in thickness. The fundamentals are the same whether you choose with a manual or electric equipment to do the task.

To get started, you need to make sure that your machine is set to the appropriate thickness. For those who have never done this before, it is recommended that you begin with the widest setting and work your way down to the thinner settings as you grow more used to the procedure.

A Rolling Pin: A Simple Yet Effective Alternative

When it comes to rolling out pasta dough, a rolling pin is a viable alternative, despite the fact that a pasta machine is the more convenient option. Although it can take a little bit more time and energy, sometimes the end product can be just as fulfilling. To prevent the food from adhering to the rolling pin, make sure there is enough of flour on it.

The Pasta Cutter: Shaping Your Creations

You are going to need a pasta cutter in order to cut your pasta dough into the necessary shapes. These are available in a variety of shapes, such as those used to cut fettuccine and spaghetti. The fact that certain pasta machines come with replaceable cutting attachments adds still another level of practicality to the process.

A Bench Scraper: Handy for Cleanup

The inclusion of a bench scraper to your arsenal of tools for creating pasta may seem like an unusual choice at first, but it is immensely handy for collecting scraps of dough, cleaning your work area, and transferring delicate noodle forms.

A Pasta Drying Rack: Ensuring Even Drying

After you have rolled and cut your pasta, a drying rack is an essential piece of equipment to have. It enables an equal drying process for your pasta, which prevents clumping and sticking throughout the cooking process. Be careful to use flour to prevent it from adhering to the surface.

Pasta Trays and Storage Containers: Preserving Freshness

Make sure to purchase pasta trays or airtight containers if you want to store freshly cooked pasta. These will preserve your products from becoming stale and will shield them from any unpleasant scents that may be present in the refrigerator.

Tips for Cooking Perfect Pasta: The Art of Seething

Now that you have all of the necessary equipment for creating pasta, it's time to go on to the next step, which is cooking it to perfection. Even while it may seem like seething pasta is a simple process, there are several subtle strategies that may bring the meals you make with pasta to a whole new level.

A Sea of Seething Water: The Pasta's Playground

The use of a huge pot filled with seething water that has been appropriately salted is the first and most important step in the process of making superb pasta. To ensure that it cooks properly, pasta need a little of breathing space. For every pound of pasta, you should use at least four to six quarts of water, as a general guideline. And don't skimp on the salt; for every gallon of water, the pasta should get around a tablespoonful of salt. This will give it a delicious flavor.

Stirring Matters: Preventing Sticking and Clumping

When you add the pasta to the water that is already seething, give it a little stir right away. Because of this, the spaghetti will not clump together and will not become stuck to the bottom of the pot. To ensure that the food cooks evenly throughout, stir it at regular intervals while it is in the oven.

The Al Dente Quest: Timing Is Key

The word "al dente" comes from the Italian phrase "to the teeth," and it is used to describe the optimal condition of cooked pasta, which is soft but still has some bite to it. Timing must be spot on in order to achieve this level of perfection. Check the directions on the box for the suggested amount of time to prepare the food, but keep in mind that they are only suggestions. The best way to appraise anything is to try it for yourself.

Reserve Pasta Water: Liquid Gold for Sauces

It is important to remember to set aside one mug of the seething water for the pasta before draining it. This starchy liquid is a miraculous element that may change and bind the sauces you make for your pasta. It is very helpful for making sauces that are smooth and emulsified, such as carbonara or aglio e olio.

Timing Matters: Sauce and Pasta in Perfect Harmony

When it comes to blending the flavors of your pasta and sauce, timing is of the utmost importance. To get the best results, you should let the sauce finish cooking the pasta. Because of this, the flavors are able to combine, and the sauce is able to attractively adhere to the pasta. When the pasta is nearly done cooking, you should have the sauce simmering and ready to go.

Sauces and Pairings: The Symphony of Flavors

Let's explore the world of pasta sauces and food pairings now that we've gone through the various pieces of equipment and methods of preparation. Choosing the correct sauce for your pasta meal can take it from average to spectacular, and understanding which flavor combinations are most successful is essential to achieving culinary mastery.

Classic Tomato Sauces: A Time-Honored Favorite

It's hard to beat the classic combination of pasta with a sauce made from tomatoes. Rich and tangy tastes make them a fan favorite, and they are available in a variety of preparations, from marinara to arrabbiata. Tomato sauces are very adaptable and go well with a broad variety of pasta types, including spaghetti, penne, and many more.

Creamy Delights: Luxurious Pasta Sauces

Pasta meals are elevated to a higher level of sophistication when topped with cream-based sauces. The silky textures and decadent tastes of Alfredo sauce, carbonara sauce, and vodka sauce have made them fan favorites. These sauces work particularly well with broader pasta forms like fettuccine and pappardelle because those noodle shapes are able to better catch and retain the creamy deliciousness of the sauce.

Pesto: The Green Elixir of Pasta

The fresh basil, garlic, pine nuts, and Parmesan cheese are the key ingredients in the flavorful and aromatic sauce known as pesto. It adds a burst of herbaceous freshness that goes very well with delicate pasta forms like linguine and filled pasta like ravioli.

Oil-Based Sauces: Simplicity at Its Finest

Oil-based sauces, such as aglio e olio (garlic and Oil), are lauded for being very straightforward and having tastes that are unadulterated. They really come into their own when combined with more delicate noodle forms like spaghetti, which reveals all of the intricacies of the individual components of the dish.

People who like seafood will be happy to know that there are a multitude of pasta sauces that highlight the abundance that can be found in the ocean. Long lengths of pasta, such as linguine or spaghetti with clams, are ideal for enjoying seafood dishes like shrimp scampi and linguine with clams because they allow the pasta to wind around the fish and convey a sense of the sea.

Pairing Pasta Shapes and Sauces: A Harmonious Match

It's not only a question of aesthetics when it comes to pairing pasta shapes with sauces; it's also about building a perfect marriage between the tastes and textures. The following is a rundown of several time-honored combinations:

Spaghetti: Ideal for tomato-based sauces, seafood, or oil-based sauces.

Fettuccine: Perfect for creamy Alfredo or carbonara sauces.

Penne: Works well with both chunky and smooth sauces, making it a versatile choice.

Ravioli: Best when paired with simple butter and herb sauces or light cream sauces.

Orzo: Excellent for salads and soups, as well as light vegetable-based sauces.

Lasagna: Traditionally used in layered dishes with rich meat and cheese sauces.

The world of pasta is filled with unfathomable possibilities that are just waiting to be discovered. You have the resources necessary to begin on a gastronomic voyage that is limitless if you know how to use the appropriate cooking equipment, cooking methods, and have an understanding of sauces and pairings. You may create a dish of comfortable spaghetti with marinara sauce or indulge in a lavish basin of fettuccine Alfredo; the world of pasta is yours to appreciate and enjoy in any way that you see fit. Now that you have all of your supplies, it's time to roll up your sleeves and get started on your pasta adventures. Good luck with your meal!

Breakfast Recipes

1. Pasta with smoked sausages and pistachios

- Serving: 3

Ingredients:

- homemade pasta or any type of pasta (15 oz)
- 15 oz smoked pork sausages, cubed
- 1/2 pint of pistachios
- 4 oz Cheddar cheese, grated
- 4 cloves of garlic
- 2 carrots, peeled and hashed
- 1/2 pint of cream
- 5 tablespoonfuls oil
- Sea salt, to taste
- pepper, to taste
- 1 bunch of parsley, hashed

Directions:

1. To roast pistachios, set an oven temperature between 250- and 270-degrees

Fahrenheit and leave them in the oven for 15 minutes, until they are gently browned and crispy. Next, use a blender or food processor to break down the pistachios.

2. Seethe the water and cook the homemade pasta for 15 minutes or follow the cooking time suggested on the packet.

3. Add 45mL Oil when the pasta is ready.

4. Blend or process the garlic, grated Cheddar cheese, cream, salt, and pepper until completely smooth and creamy.

5. To make the sausage and carrots, heat the oil in a pan and cook them over low heat for 10 minutes, or until they are golden brown. Throw the rest of the stuff into a skillet and incorporate it up.

6. Divide the spaghetti across three dishes or bowls.

7. After topping with hashed parsley, it's ready to be served.

2. Bacon And Swiss Chard Pasta

- Serving: Makes 6 servings

Ingredients

- 1 lb. linguine
- 12 ounces of bacon, sliced in half-inch diagonals.
- Half of a huge red onion, cut thinly (about 6 cups)
- 2 hefty bunches of Swiss chard, washed, and sliced (about 11-pint)
- 1 tbsp. balsamic vinegar
- 3 tbsps. extra-virgin Oil
- 160mL grated Parmesan cheese

Direction

1. Linguine should be cooked in a big saucepan of seething salted water with frequent stirring until it is soft but still has a little of bite to it. Don't throw away the cooking water; instead, set aside a mug to use later.

2. For the time being, render the fat from the bacon in a big, heavy saucepan over moderate heat until it begins to crisp, about 10 minutes. The bacon should be drained on paper towels. All except 2 tablespoonfuls of the bacon fat should be poured out of the pan. The onion should be cooked for 7 minutes over moderate

heat, or until tender. Throw in some Swiss chard. Season with salt and pepper to taste. Add the cooking liquid you set out. The chard should be soft and wilted after 4 minutes of tossing. Vinegar may be added to the mix. Warm the ingredients for a minute.

3. Combine the linguine, oil, and sauce in a huge saucepan. Stir the ingredients together and toss until everything is evenly covered. Toss the ingredients together in a big bowl, then top with cheese and bacon. Add salt and pepper to taste to the mixture.

3. Pasta with sesame seeds and peanuts

- Serving: 5

Ingredients:

- homemade pasta or any type of pasta (12 oz)
- 5 oz peanuts
- 5 tablespoonfuls sesame seeds
- 4 cloves of garlic
- 30mL unsalted butter
- half mug creams
- sunflower oil
- Sea salt
- black ground pepper

Directions:

1. Bring a pot of water to a seethe, then add the handmade pasta and cook for 15 minutes, or according to the package's instructions. Include 15 mL of oil.
2. Add 30mL sunflower oil when the pasta is ready.
3. In a pan, toast the sesame seeds and peanuts for 5 minutes and set aside.
4. Blend the garlic, peanuts, sesame seeds, peanut oil, sea salt, and black pepper in a food processor until smooth.
5. Add the sesame mixture to the melted unsalted butter and cream in a pan.
6. The pasta and sesame mixture may be tossed together and served immediately after.

- Serving: 3

Ingredients:

- homemade pasta or any type of pasta (10 oz)
- 1 avocado
- 2 garlic cloves
- 4 asparagus
- 4 oz canned beans
- 30mL lime juice
- 45mL of water
- Himalayan salt
- Oil
- black ground pepper
- Herbes de Provence
- basil

Directions:

1. Bring a pot of water to a seethe, then add the handmade pasta and cook for 15 minutes, or according to the package's instructions. Include 15 mL of oil.
2. 2 min before the pasta is ready add the asparagus and beans.
3. Add 30mL Oil when the pasta is ready.
4. Let's get to the sauce now – cut the avocado into pieces and blend it with the garlic using a blender.
5. Add the water and squeezed lime juice, incorporate well and the avocado sauce is ready!
6. Incorporate the pasta with the avocado sauce and stir well.
7. Sprinkle Herbes de Provence, Himalayan salt, pepper and basil on top.

5.   Pasta with salmon, potatoes and dill

- Serving: 3

Ingredients:

- homemade pasta or any type of pasta (12 oz)
- 20 oz salmon, cubed
- 5 potatoes, peeled and hashed
- 4 oz Cheddar cheese, grated
- 4 cloves of garlic
- 2 carrots, peeled and hashed
- 1/2 pint of cream
- 5 tablespoonfuls Oil
- Sea salt
- pepper
- 1 bunch of dill, hashed

Directions:

1. Bring a huge pot of water to a seethe, then add the handmade pasta and potatoes and cook for 15 minutes, or according to the package's instructions.
2. Add 45mL Oil when the pasta is ready.
3. Blend or process the garlic, grated Cheddar cheese, cream, salt, and pepper until completely smooth and creamy.
4. Salmon should be fried in oil over low heat for around 10 minutes. Add the other ingredients to the pan, cover, and simmer for 20 minutes.
5. Spoon the pasta into three bowls or plates.

6.   Pasta with fish and tomatoes

- Serving: 2

Ingredients:

- homemade pasta or any type of pasta (12 oz)

- 2o oz tuna, hashed
- 5 tomatoes, hashed
- 2 onions, peeled and hashed
- 30mL unsalted butter
- sunflower oil
- Sea salt
- black ground pepper

Directions:

1. Bring a pot of water to a seethe, then add the handmade pasta and cook for 15 minutes, or according to the package's instructions.
2. Add 30mL sunflower oil when the pasta is ready.
3. Put some salt and pepper on the tuna.
4. Preheat the oven and bake the tuna with the onions and tomatoes for 35 minutes.
5. Spoon the pasta into the basin and add in the tuna, onions and tomatoes.
6. Put a spoonful of spaghetti and a pinch of salt in each of two serving dishes or plates.

7. Charlotte's Tortellini Salad

- Serving: 6

Ingredients

- Cheese-stuffed tortellini, 16 ounces
- Green pepper, cut thinly (1 piece)
- 1 small red onion and 1 red bell pepper, both julienned
- 125mL sliced black olives
- 125mL crumbled feta cheese
- 1 boneless chicken breast half, cooked and sliced into thin strips
- Oil, 60 mL
- 5 mL of finely hashed lemon rind
- Lemon juice, 60 ml
- 30 mL of walnut meal
- 15mLhoney

Direction

1. Pasta should be cooked in salted water in a big pot until it is al dente, or just slightly chewy. Empty the water and let it cool in the fridge. Put it in the fridge to cool it down.
2. Honey, walnuts, lemon juice, lemon zest, and Oil are mixed together in a small basin to make the dressing. Cool in the fridge for a while.
3. Salad dish with chicken, olives, red onion, peppers, and noodles. Dress with a lemon dressing and feta cheese. Simply toss and serve.

8. Breakfast Pasta

- Serving: 4

Ingredients

- 1/2 (14 ounce) package spaghetti
- 45mL Oil, divided
- 4 eggs, beaten
- 1/2 onion, hashed
- 60mL hashed baby bella (crimini) mushrooms
- 60mL frozen peas
- 60mL shredded carrots
- 125 milliliters of freshly grated Parmesan cheese, plus salt and pepper to taste

Direction

1. Seethe a big pot with slightly salted water. In seething water, let spaghetti cook for 12 minutes, mixing from time to time till cooked completely yet firm to the bite. Allow to drain.
2. In skillet, heat a tablespoonful of oil on moderate heat; in hot oil, cook and incorporate eggs for 5 minutes, till scrambled and firm.
3. In another skillet, heat leftover 30mL of oil on moderately-high heat; sauté carrots, peas, mushrooms and onion for 10 minutes, till onion turn browned. To mixture of onion, put the pasta and toss. Put in eggs and stir thoroughly. Scatter pepper, salt and Parmesan cheese on top of pasta mixture and toss.

- Serving: 8

Ingredients

- Spaghetti, one 16-ounce packet
- Beef, ground, one pound
- One sliced onion
- Meatless spaghetti sauce, one 32-ounce jar
- Seasoning salt, 1/2 teaspoon
- 2 eggs
- 80mL grated Parmesan cheese
- 5 tbsps. butter, melted
- 1-pint small curd cottage cheese, divided
- Approximately 4 cups of shredded mozzarella cheese.

Direction

1. Bring the oven temperature up to 175 degrees Celsius (around 350 degrees Fahrenheit). Lightly grease a 9-by-13-inch baking dish.
2. Put a lot of lightly salted water on to seethe. Pasta should be cooked for around 12 minutes with occasional stirring until al dente and drained.
3. Put the steak and onion in a huge pan and cook them over moderate heat. Stirring occasionally, brown the steak and get it to a transparent softness before draining it takes around 7 minutes. Season with salt and add spaghetti sauce.
4. Cream together the butter, Parmesan cheese, and eggs in a huge bowl. Incorporate the spaghetti in till it is well covered. Put half of the spaghetti mixture in the dish and bake as directed. Sprinkle half of the cottage cheese and mozzarella on top. Cover it with some beef sauce. Cover with aluminum foil and proceed to add more layers.
5. Bake for 40mins in the 350°Fahrenheit or 175°C preheated oven. Take off the foil and bake for another 20-25mins until the cheese melts and lightly browned.

10. Pasta with pork sausages and tomatoes

- Serving: 2

Ingredients:

- homemade pasta or any type of pasta (15 oz)
- 5 medium pork sausages, hashed
- 5 oz sundried tomatoes
- 1/2 pint of Cheddar cheese, grated
- 2 onions
- 30mL unsalted butter
- 5 tablespoonfuls mayonnaise
- 1/2 pint of cream
- 5 tablespoonfuls sunflower oil
- sea salt, for flavor; black peppercorns, for spice

Directions:

1. Warm some water and soak the dried tomatoes for around 10 minutes.
2. Bring water to a seethe and cook the handmade pasta according to the package directions (about 15 minutes). Put in 15 mL of oil.
3. When the pasta is done cooking, pour in 30 mL of sunflower oil.
4. To make caramelized onions, chop them and cook them over low heat for 10 minutes. Throw in several pork sausages and cook them slowly for ten minutes.
5. Blend the cream, tomatoes, mayonnaise, Himalayan salt, and freshly ground black pepper in a food processor until completely smooth.
6. Put some spaghetti in a basin and toss it with the rest of the ingredients.
7. Grate some Cheddar cheese and sprinkle it on top. To serve, just ladle the pasta onto bowls or plates and top with a generous helping of the seasoning.

11. Pasta with lamb and potatoes

- Serving: 3

Ingredients:

- homemade pasta or any type of pasta (15 oz)
- 20 oz lamb, cubed
- 4 medium potatoes, peeled and hashed
- 5 cloves of garlic
- 10 oz Parmesan cheese, grated
- 5 tablespoonfuls mayonnaise
- Sea salt
- 5 tablespoonfuls Oil
- black ground pepper

Directions:

1. Bring a pot of water to a seethe, then add the handmade pasta and cook for 15 minutes, or according to the package's instructions. Include 15 mL of oil. The potatoes should be cooked for around 15 minutes.
2. In a food processor, combine the mayonnaise, Parmesan cheese, Sea salt, and black pepper and pulse until smooth.
3. For around 40 minutes over moderate heat, cook the lamb cubes in the oil until they are golden brown.
4. Add the spaghetti and the rest of the ingredients to the pan and cover for 10 minutes to simmer.
5. Place a spoonful of spaghetti and a pinch of salt and pepper on each dish.

12. Pasta with the veal, chicken and pineapples

- Serving: 4

Ingredients:

- homemade pasta or any type of pasta (20 oz)

- 25 oz veal, ground
- 15 oz chicken, ground
- 1-pint of pineapple, cubed
- 2 red onions, peeled and hashed
- 4 oz unsalted butter
- 10 crushed cloves of garlic
- 8 tablespoonfuls mayonnaise
- sunflower oil
- Sea salt
- black ground pepper
- Herbs de Provence
- soy sauce
- dried basil
- 1 bunch fresh hashed parsley

Directions:

1. Whisk together the basil, garlic, herbs, salt, and black pepper. Incorporate the spices with the veal and chicken. Marinate the beef in the soy sauce for as long as possible, preferably overnight in the fridge but at least a few hours at room temperature.
2. Prepare the handmade pasta by bringing water to a seethe and seething it for 15 minutes, or for the amount of time specified on the package. Increase the amount by 15 mL oil.
3. The onions should be hashed, the oil heated, and then fried over a low heat for 10 minutes, until they are golden brown and caramelized. Cook the veal and chicken for 30 minutes in a frying pan before switching to a stewing pan for 10 minutes.
4. Pasta should be mixed with the meat, onions, garlic, mayonnaise, sunflower oil, soy sauce, Sea salt, black ground pepper, oregano, and Herbs de Provence. Include the pineapples.
5. Put some pasta and meat on each dish and sprinkle some hashed parsley on top.

13. Old Fashioned Mac 'n Cheese

- Serving: 4

Ingredients

- 4 cups cooked macaroni
- 30mL butter, melted
- 375mL Cheddar cheese, cubed
- 375mL Jack cheese, cubed
- 1/2-pint Kikkoman Panko Bread Crumbs
- 1 teaspoonful seasoned salt
- 1/2 teaspoonful black pepper
- 2 eggs, beaten
- 1-pint Kikkoman PEARL Original Soymilk

Direction

1. Prepare the oven by preheating to 350°F. Incorporate seasonings, cheese and macaroni. Transfer in an 8x13-inch baking dish. Incorporate soymilk and eggs then place on macaroni. Sprinkle a thin layer of Panko bread crumbs on top. For a golden crust, bake at 400 degrees for 40 minutes.

14. Pesto Polenta Lasagna

- Serving: 8

Ingredients

- 1 (18-ounce) container of polenta, sliced to a thickness of 14 inch
- One-half of a standard 24-ounce jar of bottled marinara
- 60mL pesto
- 60mL pine nuts
- 1/2-pint shredded mozzarella cheese

Direction

1. Prepare a baking dish by preheating the oven to 375 degrees Fahrenheit (190 degrees Celsius). Spray some oil in an 11-by-7-by-2-inch baking dish and set it aside.
2. Put a thin layer of pesto on the bottom, and then a layer of polenta on top. Spread half of the sauce over the polenta. Create a second layer of polenta and sauce on top of the first.
3. Let it bake, uncovered, for 25 minutes. Switch on your broiler. Put some pine nuts and cheese on the top of the polenta and set it into the broiler. Continue to broil until the nuts are already crispy and the cheese turns to brown.

15. Pasta with apricots and raisins

- Serving: 4

Ingredients:

- homemade pasta or any type of pasta (12 oz)
- 1/2 pint of cashews
- 1/2 pint of raisins
- 1/2 pint of apricots
- 30mL unsalted butter
- 1/2 pint of cream
- 45mL sunflower oil

Directions:

1. Bring a pot of water to a seethe, then add the handmade pasta and cook for 15 minutes, or according to the package's instructions.
2. When the pasta is done, drizzle with 30 mL of sunflower oil.
3. The apricots and raisins should be washed and soaked in the hot water for about 10 minutes.
4. In a preheated oven between 250- and 270-degrees Fahrenheit, roast the cashews for 10 minutes, or until they are lightly browned and crispy. The cashews should next be ground in a blender or food processor.

5. Melt the unsalted butter and cream in a pan, then stir in the dried fruit.
6. When ready to serve, just divide the pasta among dishes and top with a dollop of the apricot-raisin combination and some cashews.

16. Pasta with eggplant, champignons and bread

- Serving: 3

Ingredients:

- homemade pasta or any type of pasta (15 oz)
- 1 eggplant
- 10 oz bread, hashed
- 5 oz freshly hashed champignons (mushrooms)
- 2 onions, peeled and hashed
- 7 crushed cloves of garlic
- 4 tablespoonfuls marinara sauce
- 30mL pumpkin seeds oil
- mug of water
- sea salt
- black ground pepper
- Herbs de Provence
- 1 bunch fresh hashed parsley

Directions:

1. Bring a pot of water to a seethe, then add the handmade pasta and cook for 15 minutes, or according to the package's instructions. Toss in 15 mL of pumpkin seed oil.
2. Add 30mL pumpkin seeds oil when the pasta is ready. Later we will use the water from the seethed pasta.
3. Now that the eggplant has been cubed, we can begin making the sauce.
4. Toss the eggplant with the salt in a colander. Just wait 15 minutes.
5. Fry the onions in oil over moderate heat until they are translucent and caramelized. In a hot frying pan, toast the bread for 10 minutes.
6. Add the eggplant, garlic, champignons and fry until clear and golden brown.
7. Pour the water from the seethed pasta and stew for 5 min, and then set aside and

cover for 5 min. Add in the Herbs de Provence, some salt and pepper.

8. Place the pasta into the sauce, stir well and sprinkle the parsley on top.

17. Pasta with pumpkin and cheese

- Serving: 3

Ingredients:

- pasta or any type of pasta (12 oz)
- 20 oz pumpkin, hashed
- 5mL orange zest, minced
- 4 tomatoes
- 1/2 pint of Gouda cheese, grated
- 2 onions
- 5 crushed cloves of garlic
- sunflower oil
- sea salt
- black ground pepper

Directions:

1. Bring a huge pot of water to a seethe, then add the pasta and cook for the specified amount of time, usually 15 minutes. Put in 15 mL of oil.
2. Prepare the onions for the sauce immediately.
3. Stirring constantly, cook the garlic and onions in the oil over low heat for about 5 minutes, until the onions are transparent and caramelized.
4. Put in the pumpkin and cook for 5 minutes.
5. Put in the orange zest and let it sit covered for 10 minutes.
6. Tomatoes, after being cut, should be added to a skillet and cooked for about 5 minutes.
7. The spaghetti should be added and stirred in before the Gouda is sprinkled on top.
8. Put the spaghetti in four dishes or plates and sprinkle little salt and pepper on top of each serving.

- Serving: 4

Ingredients:

- homemade pasta or any type of pasta (around 15-17 oz)
- 5 oz fresh broccoli
- 1 can of canned green peas
- 1 can of canned corn
- 3 crushed cloves of garlic
- 1 peeled and sliced onion
- 2 peeled and sliced carrots
- 1 fresh tomato
- 30mL of flour
- 15mLpumpkin seeds oil
- 4 tablespoonfuls tomato paste
- 1/2-pint water
- 8 tablespoonfuls mayonnaise
- salt
- red ground pepper
- 1 bunch fresh hashed parsley

Directions:

1. Bring a pot of water to a seethe, then add the handmade pasta and cook for 15 minutes, or according to the package's instructions. Include 15 mL of oil. Carrots and broccoli should be seethed until they are halfway done.
2. To make a golden-brown onion, chop it up, heat some oil, and fried it for 2 minutes.
3. Garlic should be fried in the same oil for 1 minute over moderate heat.
4. Tomato paste and water should be combined first, then flour should be added and well mixed.
5. For 15 minutes, while stirring occasionally, bring the sauce to a seethe.
6. Cook the sauce for a further 12 minutes after adding the canned green peas and corn.

7. Chop up some fresh parsley and add it to the sauce.
8. Carrots, after seething, may be added to the sauce after being cut into bite-sized pieces. Incorporate in the mayonnaise, salt, and cayenne. Leave the sauce uncovered for 5-10 minutes to allow the flour to permeate into the sauce.
9. Put some pasta in each dish or on each plate, and then add some of the sauce to each. Slice the tomatoes and serve them beside the spaghetti. Combine the oil from the pumpkin seeds with the parsley.

19. Pasta with cheese and basil

- Serving: 3

Ingredients:

- homemade pasta or any type of pasta (10 oz)
- 8 crushed cloves of garlic
- 5mL garlic powder
- 30mL dried basil
- 10 oz gorgonzola cheese, grated
- 30mL lemon juice
- Oil
- black ground pepper
- Herbes de Provence
- hashed chives
- sea salt, to taste

Directions:

1. Seethe the water and cook the homemade pasta for 15 minutes or follow the cooking time suggested on the packet. Add 15mLoil.
2. Add 30mL Oil when the pasta is ready.
3. Pour the squeezed lemon juice and incorporate the pasta with the garlic, garlic powder and stir well.
4. Sprinkle the Herbs de Provence, Sea salt and black ground pepper.
5. Grate the gorgonzola cheese on top and dollop each basin or plate with the chives and basil and you are free to serve!

- Serving: 8

Ingredients

- One pound of rotini pasta
- 30mL Oil
- 1-pint hashed kale, or to taste
- 5mL garlic powder
- 5mL garlic salt
- 1 teaspoonful chipotle pepper powder
- Vegetable broth, one 14-ounce can
- 2 cans of cannellini beans, 15 ounces each
- 125mL shredded Mexican cheese blend, or to taste

Direction

1. Bring a huge saucepan of lightly salted water to a seethe, then add the rotini and simmer for 8 minutes, or until tender but still firm to the biting.
2. Oil should be heated in a huge pan over moderate heat. Incorporate the chipotle pepper powder, garlic salt, and garlic powder with the kale and add it to the skillet. To wilt kale, cook it for 1–2 minutes while stirring often.
3. Vegetable broth is added to the kale, along with the cannellini beans. For the next 7 or 8 minutes, while tossing the mixture often, cook until the beans are tender.
4. Cooked rotini with the bean mixture and greens for 1 to 2 minutes, stirring occasionally. Shredded Mexican cheese should be sprinkled on top.

Lunch Recipes

21. Chickpea Pasta with Lemony Parsley Pesto

- Serving: 2

Ingredients

- 4 ounces of penne pasta, such as chickpea penne or another kind (approximately 1 1/4 cups dry)
- About 1 bunch of flat-leaf parsley (four cups, loosely packed) and additional for decoration.
- 3 cloves garlic
- ⅓ mug extra-virgin Oil
- 1 teaspoonful lemon zest
- 30mL lemon juice
- ½ teaspoonful kosher salt
- ¼ teaspoonful ground black pepper
- 1½ cups roasted root vegetables (see associated recipe)

Direction:

1. Cook the pasta following the package instructions, then drain well.
2. In the meantime, in a food processor, incorporate together the garlic and parsley, then pulse for around 10 times, until it becomes uniformly hashed. Add pepper, salt, lemon juice and oil and puree for about 15 seconds until just blended; it must be chunky.
3. The roasted root vegetables may be reheated in the microwave for one minute in a microwave-safe dish. Alternately, heat the veggies through by cooking them in a huge frying pan with 1 teaspoon of extra-virgin Oil over moderate heat for 2 to 4 minutes while stirring constantly.
4. Stir the lemon zest, veggies, and pesto into the heated pasta, then top with parsley, if using.

22. Tuna Antipasto Salad Basin

- Serving: 8

Ingredients

- Greens for a salad, about 8 cups worth, cleaned and torn into little pieces.
- Garbanzo beans, one 15-ounce can, drained and rinsed
- 1 (15 oz.) can whole black olives, pitted and drained
- 1 drained and quartered container of marinated artichoke hearts (14 ounces)
- 8 ounces of cooked and cooled shell pasta 2 cans of tuna, 5 ounces each
- One cucumber, cut thinly
- 1/2-pint hashed tomato
- 375mL Italian-style salad dressing, or to taste

Direction

1. In a big bowl, incorporate tomato, cucumber, shell pasta, tuna, artichoke hearts, black olives, garbanzo beans and salad greens. Keep it covered and let salad chill in the refrigerator till lettuce becomes crisp and mixture becomes chilled no less than 2 hours.
2. Incorporate salad with salad dressing instantly prior to serving.

23. Penne Pesto Pasta Salad

- Serving: 8

Ingredients

- 1 (8 ounce) package truRoots® Ancient Grains Organic Penne
- 125 mL of ready-to-eat fresh basil pesto
- 8 ounces of mozzarella pearls (perline)* 1 pint of grape or cherry tomatoes (halved) 60 milliliters of grated Parmesan
- Black olives, one (2.25 ounce) can, cut and drained
- Garnish with sprigs of fresh basil (optional)

Direction

1. Pasta should be cooked in salted seething water for 7–9 minutes in a big saucepan until it is tender but still firm. Drain.
2. Pesto and spaghetti may be mixed together in a big bowl. Add the olives, Parmesan, tomatoes, and mozzarella and incorporate well. Keep refrigerated until ready to serve. The basil sprigs may be used for garnish if you choose. Enjoy!

24. Lemon Garlic Sardine Fettuccine for Two

- Serving: 2

Ingredients

- Whole wheat fettuccine, 4 ounces
- Half a mug of fresh breadcrumbs (see Tip), ideally whole wheat 30 milliliters of fresh lemon juice Two hashed garlic cloves
- ½ teaspoonful freshly ground pepper
- ¼ teaspoonful salt
- 1/4 mug hashed fresh parsley 1 can sardines (3 or 4 ounces), boneless and skinless, ideally in tomato sauce
- Thinly shaved Parmesan cheese (around 30 mL)

Direction

1. Seethe big pot of water. Follow package directions to cook pasta or for 8-10 minutes till just tender; drain.
2. Meanwhile, in a small, nonstick pan, heat 1 tablespoonful of oil over moderate heat. For 20 seconds, stirring constantly, sauté the garlic until it is sizzling and aromatic but not brown. Combine oil and garlic in a huge bowl.
3. One tablespoonful of oil should be heated in a pan over moderate heat. Stir in breadcrumbs, and heat for another 3–5 minutes, or until they are golden and crisp. Affix to dish.
4. Stir salt, pepper and lemon juice into garlic oil. Add pasta, Parmesan, parsley and sardines into bowl; incorporate gently to combine. Sprinkle breadcrumbs over to serve.

25. Curry Chicken Pasta Salad

- Serving: 6

Ingredients

- Five pieces of chicken breast
- 1 (8-ounce) box of shell pasta
- One-half mug of low-calorie mayonnaise
- 1/4 mug of plain, nonfat yogurt
- Curry powder, to taste (1 teaspoon minimum)
- 1/2 (10 ounce) thawed container of frozen peas 4 sliced radishes
- 2 sliced green onions

Direction

1. In a huge saucepan, bring some gently salted water to a seethe. The chicken breasts should be cooked for 12-15 minutes in the seething water, or until the juices run clear and the flesh is no longer pink in the middle. Inserting a thermometer into the middle should provide a reading of at least 74 degrees Celsius (165 degrees

Fahrenheit). To quicken the cooling process, you may rinse the chicken in cold water, then chop it into bite-sized pieces and place them in the fridge.

2. A huge saucepan of lightly salted water should be brought to a seethe. Cook shell pasta in a huge pot of salted seething water for 8 minutes, stirring occasionally. It should be al dente. Once the paste has cooled, drain it and rinse it under cold water. Revitalize the draining system.

3. Combine the curry powder, yogurt, and mayonnaise in a huge basin and incorporate well. Toss in some sliced green onions, sliced radishes, frozen peas, shredded chicken, and chilled spaghetti and incorporate to combine.

4. Cover the basin with plastic wrap and place it in the fridge for at least three hours before serving.

26. Marinated Chicken and Pasta Salad

- Serving: 6

Ingredients

- 45mL soy sauce
- 30mL honey
- 30mL tomato sauce
- 30mL plum sauce
- 15mLWorcestershire sauce
- 1 teaspoonful sesame seeds
- 1 teaspoonful hashed fresh basil
- 3 skinless, boneless chicken breast halves
- 1-pint elbow macaroni
- 30mL Oil
- 125mL low-fat mayonnaise
- 125mL fat free sour cream
- 1 teaspoonful coarse grained prepared mustard
- 15mLhoney
- 15mLtomato sauce
- 1 teaspoonful Worcestershire sauce
- Sharp Cheddar cheese, shredded (60 mL)
- Peel, remove seed, and thinly slice 1 avocado.
- Cashews, 125 mL

Direction

1. Basil, sesame seeds, 15mL Worcestershire sauce, 30mL plum sauce, 30mL tomato sauce, 30mL honey, and 45mL soy sauce should be combined in a big dish. To coat the chicken, put it in and turn.
2. Marinate for at least an hour in the fridge.
3. Bring a big saucepan of lightly salted water to a seethe. When the water returns to a seethe, add the pasta and cook for 8 to 10 minutes, or until al dente.
4. Oil should be heated in a pan over moderate heat. Place the chicken in the oven and roast it until the juices flow clear. Use paper towels for draining. Once it's cooled, cut it into manageable pieces.
5. Combine in a huge basin the 1 teaspoonful Worcestershire sauce, 15mLtomato sauce, 15mLhoney, mustard, sour cream, and mayonnaise. Add in Cheddar cheese, chicken and cooked pasta. Gradually incorporate in sliced avocado and cashews just before serving.

27. Pasta with Gruyère cheese and champignons

- Serving: 4

Ingredients:

- homemade pasta or any type of pasta (around 15-17 oz)
- 10 oz freshly hashed champignons (mushrooms)
- 5 oz cauliflower
- 4 hashed garlic cloves
- 15mLgarlic powder
- 2 onions, hashed
- 30mL of flour
- 1/2-pint milk or cream
- 1/2 pint of Gruyère cheese, grated
- Oil
- half mug red wine
- sea salt, for flavor; black peppercorns, for spice
- Herbs de Provence

Directions:

1. Seethe the water and cook the homemade pasta for 15 minutes or follow the cooking time suggested on the packet. Add 15mLOil. In parallel, seethe the cauliflower to half-cooked.
2. When the pasta is ready add 30mL Oil. Later we will use the water from the seethed pasta.
3. Prepare the sauce by dicing the onions and mushrooms.
4. Fry the onions in hot oil until they are brown and caramelized. Follow that by incorporating the minced garlic and garlic powder.
5. Add in the champignons and flour to fry on a low heat for 20 minutes.
6. Pour the water from the seethed pasta and red wine and stew for 5 minutes with the lid closed.
7. Cook for 5 minutes after adding the milk/cream.
8. Cook the cauliflower in the sauce for 5 minutes with the lid on once it has been cooked and hashed. Put in some salt and pepper and the Herbs de Provence. The sauce needs the Gruyeres cheese added to it. Add the spaghetti to the sauce and incorporate well.

28. Pasta with goose and oranges

- Serving: 4

Ingredients:

- homemade pasta or any type of pasta (12 oz)
- 20 oz goose, cubed
- 4 oranges, peeled and hashed
- 1/2 pint of Parmesan cheese
- 1/2 pint of walnuts, ground
- 4 cloves of garlic
- 30mL unsalted butter
- 1/2 pint of cream
- 5 tablespoonfuls Oil
- Sea salt
- black ground pepper

Directions:

1. Bring a pot of water to a seethe, then add the handmade pasta and cook for 15 minutes, or according to the package's instructions. Include 15 mL of oil.
2. When the pasta has finished cooking, toss with 4 tablespoonfuls of Oil.
3. Blend the cream, garlic, walnuts, Parmesan cheese, sea salt, and ground black pepper until completely smooth and creamy in a food processor.
4. Just pour in 45 mL of Oil and stir to combine.
5. Heat the oil in a pan over moderate heat, and cook the geese for 30 minutes. Then stir in the orange juice, cream, and unsalted butter. Stew with the lid on for 15 minutes over low heat.
6. Toss the pasta with the cream-pesto sauce, then add the goose. Place a spoonful of spaghetti and a pinch of seasoning on each dish. You are now at liberty to serve.

29. Pasta with anchovy and cucumbers

- Serving: 6

Ingredients:

- homemade pasta or any type of pasta (15 oz)
- 1 can of drained anchovies
- 5 cloves of garlic
- 10 oz Parmesan cheese, grated
- 2 cucumbers
- 5 tablespoonfuls mayonnaise
- Sea salt
- Oil
- black ground pepper

Directions:

1. Bring water to a seethe and cook the handmade pasta according to the package directions (about 15 minutes). Put in 15 mL of oil.
2. Blend the anchovies, garlic, mayonnaise, Parmesan cheese, Sea salt, and black pepper until smooth in a food processor.

3. Toss the spaghetti with the grated cucumbers and serve.
4. To serve, toss the spaghetti with the anchovy sauce and sprinkle the cucumbers on top.

30. Pasta with crab, shrimps and tomatoes

- Serving: 6

Ingredients:

- homemade pasta or any type of pasta (15 oz)
- 10 oz of crab meat
- 4 oz shrimps
- 5 oz sundried tomatoes
- 4 oz Parmesan cheese, grated
- 2 onions
- 30mL unsalted butter
- 5 tablespoonfuls mayonnaise
- half mug creams
- sunflower oil
- Himalayan salt
- black ground pepper

Directions:

1. Bring a pot of water to a seethe, then add the handmade pasta and cook for 15 minutes, or according to the package's instructions. Include 15 mL of oil.
2. When the pasta is done, drizzle with 30 mL of sunflower oil.
3. To get the onions to a golden-brown color, chop them and fried them on low heat for 10 minutes.
4. To soften the shrimp and crab flesh, seethe them and then pulse them in a blender.
5. Blend the shrimp, crab meat, mayonnaise, Himalayan salt, and black pepper in a food processor until completely smooth.
6. Butter and heavy cream should be melted together in a pan.
7. Transfer the pasta to a basin and stir in the hashed onions, sundried tomatoes, cream, and crab.
8. Sprinkle with the grated Parmesan cheese on top and you are free to serve!

- Serving: 8

Ingredients

- 5 quarts water
- 1 (16 ounce) package rotini pasta
- 1 60mLs tomato juice
- 1 1/30mL Oil
- 15mLred wine vinegar
- 1 1/5mL chili powder
- 3/4 teaspoonful paprika
- 1/2 teaspoonful salt
- 1/4 teaspoonful ground black pepper
- 125 milliliters of grated Parmesan cheese 125 milliliters of fried corn kernels
- 80mL of freshly hashed cilantro
- 60 ml of green onion bits
- 30 mL of hashed red bell pepper
- Pepper, green, 30 mL
- 1 cooked breast without bones, hashed

Direction

1. Put the Rotini pasta in a pot of seething water. Prepare per the directions on the box. Drain the cooked pasta and run it under cold water to cool it down.
2. Oil, tomato juice, vinegar, paprika, chili powder, black pepper, and salt should all be combined in a bowl. Refrigerate for 2 to 4 hours to blend flavors, then pour over spaghetti.
3. Incorporate together corn, cilantro, scallions, Parmesan cheese, hashed chicken breast, green and red bell peppers, and red and green bell peppers. Combine, then refrigerate for at least 8 hours, preferably overnight, uncovered.

- Serving: 6

Ingredients

- 1 box of rotini pasta, 8 ounces
- Chicken (1 pint), hashed (1 stalk celery), roasted red peppers (from a jar), drained (save juice), and hashed (1 green onion), thinly sliced (125 mL) mayonnaise (like Hellmann's®/Best Foods®)
- To taste, or 30mL of spicy pepper sauce (like Frank's Red-hot®)
- 30mL crumbled Gorgonzola cheese
- 1 teaspoonful Worcestershire sauce

Direction

1. Bring a huge saucepan of lightly salted water to a seethe. Cook the rotini according to the package directions, usually 8 minutes.
2. In the salad bowl, combine 1 tbsp. of the reserved roasted red pepper juice, roasted red pepper, celery, chicken and pasta. In another bowl, whisk together Worcestershire sauce, Gorgonzola cheese, hot sauce and mayonnaise till combined completely. Add the dressing on the pasta mixture and coat by tossing gently. Keep chilled prior to serving.

33. Shrimp Vermicelli Salad

- Serving: 10

Ingredients

- Vermicelli pasta, one pound
- 1 lb. of shrimp, cooked
- 2 celery sticks, hashed
- 15mLhashed fresh parsley
- 1 clove garlic, crushed
- 1 teaspoonful dried thyme

- 1/2-pint mayonnaise
- 60mL grated Parmesan cheese
- salt and pepper to taste

Direction

1. Bring a big saucepan of water to a seethe and season it gently with salt. Pasta should be added and cooked for 8-10 minutes, then strained.
2. Once the pasta has cooled, incorporate in the spices, salt, Parmesan, mayonnaise, thyme, garlic, parsley, celery, and cooked shrimp. Wait until cooled to serve,

34. Chicken Paprikash

- Serving: 4

Ingredients

- 3 eggs, beaten
- 125mL water
- 2 1/1-pint all-purpose flour
- 2 tsps. salt
- 60mL butter
- 1 1/2 lbs. bone-in chicken pieces, with skin
- 1 medium onion, hashed
- Water, 375mL
- 1 tablespoonful paprika
- 1 teaspoon of ground black pepper 1/2 teaspoon of salt
- 2 tablespoonfuls of flour of any kind
- Sour cream, 125mL

Direction

1. Fill a big saucepan with water and bring it to a rapid seethe over high heat. In a huge dish, incorporate125 mL of water, the eggs, and 2 teaspoonfuls of salt. Add the flour gradually to make a thick batter (about 2 11 pint). Use one spoon to scoop out some batter, and then use the other to scrape it into the pot of seething water.

Do this until you have a few dumplings in the oven. For about 10 minutes, or until they float to the top, cook the dumplings. Gather them out of the water and let them dry in a strainer. Then, wash it off with some warm water.

2. In a huge pan, melt the butter over moderate heat and add the chicken. Turn once while cooking for a little browning. Cook the onion for 5–8 minutes in the skillet. Pepper, salt, and paprika may be added to the 375 mL of water. Wait 10 minutes, or until a fork inserted into the center of a piece of chicken comes out clean. The chicken should be removed from the pan and kept at a warm temperature.

3. Sour cream and two tablespoonfuls of flour should be combined and then stirred into the onion mixture in the pan. To thicken, bring the ingredients to a seethe while stirring constantly.

4. Serve the dumplings with the sour cream and onion combination by placing them in a serving bowl.

35. Christmas Tortellini & Spinach Soup

- Serving: 6 servings.

Ingredients

- Two 14-and-a-half-ounce cans 1 box of vegetable broth (9 oz.) cheese tortellini, or any other kind of tortellini, stored in the refrigerator
- White kidney beans, cannellini beans, or both, one 15-ounce can with the liquid drained
- 1 can (14-1/2 oz.) Hashed Italian tomatoes, no liquid added
- 1/4 tsp. salt
- 1/8 tsp. pepper
- 1 ½ pints fresh baby spinach
- 3 tbsps. minced fresh basil
- 60mL shredded Asiago cheese

Direction

1. In a huge pot, bring the broth to a seethe. Add the tortellini and reduce the heat to maintain a gentle simmer for 5 minutes. Add seasonings and bring to a simmer with the tomatoes and beans. Tortellini should be cooked for a further 4–5 minutes, or until tender.

2. Basil and frozen spinach should be combined and cooked until thawed. Sprinkle some cheese on top of each serving and serve immediately.

36. Creamy Tuna-noodle Casserole

- Serving: 6 servings.

Ingredients

- Noodles: 5 cups dry
- Frozen peas, half a pint
- 1 can (10-3/4 oz.) Cream of mushroom condensed soup with reduced fat and sodium, undiluted
- Reduced-fat sour cream, 1/2-pint
- Parmesan cheese, grated, 160 ml
- Two-thirds of a mug of 2% milk
- One-fourth of a teaspoon of salt
- 2 cans (5 oz. each) flaked and drained light tuna from water
- Hashed Onion, 60mL
- Green pepper, 60 mL, hashed finely
- Crumbs, 125 mL soft bread
- 1 tablespoonful of melted butter

Direction

1. The oven has to be preheated to 350 degrees. Noodles should be prepared according to package specifications for al dente and peas should be added in the last minutes of cooking before being drained.
2. Meanwhile, in a huge bowl, stir together the salt, cheese, sour cream, milk, and soup; then stir in the pepper, onion, and tuna. Toss the noodles and peas together.
3. Transfer to a baking dish 11x7 inches in size and coat with cooking spray. Incorporate bread crumbs and melted butter in a small dish, then sprinkle on top. Bake uncovered for 25-30 minutes, checking occasionally.

- Serving: Serves 6

Ingredients

- Cornstarch, 1 1/2 tablespoonfuls
- Dry mustard, 1 1/2 teaspoonfuls
- Curry powder, 1.5 teaspoonfuls
- 560mLs whole milk
- 6 tbsps. (3/4 stick) butter
- 560mLs (packed) grated sharp cheddar cheese (about 10 oz.)
- 8 oz. small elbow macaroni, freshly cooked
- 2 1/1-pint fresh breadcrumbs made from 8 oz. trimmed sourdough bread

Direction

1. To preheat the oven, choose the "bake" setting and heat the oven to 350 degrees Fahrenheit. In a glass baking dish that's 8 by 8 by 2, spread some butter. Combine cornstarch, dry mustard, and curry powder (one teaspoon each) in a big, heavy pot. Slowly add in the milk and stir. After the sauce has come to a seethe, whisk in the remaining 2 tablespoonfuls of butter and continue cooking for another minute over moderate heat. Just take it out of the oven. Stir in the cheese until a smooth consistency is reached. Blend in the macaroni. Salt and pepper the mixture, then lay it out in the prepared dish.
2. The remaining butter should be melted over moderate heat in a big, heavy skillet. Incorporate in the dry mustard and curry powder that made up the remaining half teaspoon. Whisk in the breadcrumbs and cook for 8 minutes, until they are brown and crisp.
3. Put the crumbs on top of the mac and cheese. Cook for 30 minutes, or until bubbly around the edges and hot in the center. It's best to serve the concoction when it's still piping hot.

- Serving: 3

Ingredients:

- homemade pasta or any type of pasta (12 oz)
- 5 medium and smoked beef sausages, hashed
- 4 oz Cheddar cheese, grated
- 4 cloves of garlic
- 2 eggs
- 1/2 pint of cream
- 5 tablespoonfuls Oil
- Sea salt, to taste
- Chili pepper, to taste

Directions:

1. Bring a pot of water to a seethe, then add the handmade pasta and cook for 15 minutes, or according to the package's instructions. Include 15 mL of oil.
2. When the pasta is done cooking, add 4 tablespoonfuls of Oil.
3. Put the garlic, salt, and pepper in a blender and blend until smooth.
4. Sausages should be fried in oil over low heat for 20 minutes.
5. Use a hand mixer to combine the egg yolks and cream. Salt and garlic should be added.
6. Pasta, eggs cream, and sausages should all be cooked together in a pan. Stew with the lid on for 10 minutes over low heat.
7. Sprinkle the cheese on top, and it's ready to be served.

Dinner Recipes

39. Pasta with chicken livers and cheese

- Serving: 3

Ingredients:

- homemade pasta or any type of pasta (12 oz)
- 15 oz chicken livers
- 8 bacon slices
- 4 oz Cheddar cheese, grated
- 4 cloves of garlic
- 4 oz unsalted butter
- 2 eggs
- Half a pint of milk, a mug of cream
- 5 tablespoonfuls Oil
- Sea salt, to taste
- Pepper, to taste
- 1 bunch parsley, hashed

Directions:

1. Seethe the water and cook the homemade pasta for 15 minutes or follow the cooking time suggested on the packet. Add 4 tablespoonfuls Oil when the pasta is ready.
2. Soak the chicken livers in milk for around 2 hours and then slice them.
3. Bake the bacon pieces on a baking sheet for 15 minutes at 300°F to 310°F. Keep the bacon fat for later.
4. Melt the butter in a pan over moderate heat. Put the chicken livers in a pan and turn the heat to medium-low.
5. Blend or process the garlic, salt, and pepper until a smooth and creamy consistency is reached.
6. Use a hand mixer to combine the egg yolks and cream.
7. Spoon the pasta into the skillet and add the cream sauce and the garlic mixture. Add in the livers.
8. Place bacon slices on top and pour the melted bacon grease.
9. Place a serving of pasta on each dish or bowl, and then sprinkle each serving with a little bit of minced parsley and cheddar cheese.

40. Pasta with salmon

- Serving: 3

Ingredients:

- homemade pasta or any type of pasta (12 oz)
- 15 oz smoked salmon, sliced
- 1/2 pint of walnuts
- 1/2 pint of Gouda cheese, grated
- 4 cloves of garlic
- 2 carrots, peeled and hashed
- 1/2 pint of cream
- Oil, about 5 tablespoonfuls
- To season with sea salt and pepper
- 1 bundle of hashed parsley

Directions:

1. To roast walnuts, set oven temperature to 250°F to 270°F and leave them in the oven for 15 minutes, until they are gently browned and crispy. Next, use a blender or food processor to break down the walnuts.
2. Bring water to a seethe and cook the handmade pasta according to the package directions (about 15 minutes).
3. When the pasta is done cooking, add 45 mL of Oil.
4. In a blender or food processor, combine the garlic, Gouda cheese, cream, salt, and pepper until completely smooth and creamy.
5. Carrots should be fried in oil over low heat for about 10 minutes, or until caramelized. Put the remaining ingredients into the pan and incorporate them together.
6. Divide the spaghetti across three dishes or bowls.
7. Sprinkle the hashed parsley on top and you are free to serve.

41. Eggless Pasta

- Serving: 4

Ingredients

- 1-mugof polenta
- One-half teaspoon of salt
- 500mL of hot water

Direction

1. In a huge basin, combine the flour and salt. Incorporate with hot water to make a firm dough. Add more water if the dough seems dry.
2. Shape into a ball, then transfer to a floured work surface and knead until smooth and elastic, about 10 minutes. Take 20 minutes to rest the dough.
3. Roll out dough using a pasta machine or rolling pin; use just a quarter of the dough at a time. Cover those around you to prevent them from drying out. By hand, roll to a thickness of 1/16 inch. If you're using a machine, use the third to last option.
4. Shape spaghetti anyway you choose.

5. To prepare new noodles, seethe them in salted water for three to five minutes, then drain.

42. Fettuccine Con Carciofi

- Serving: Makes 6 servings

Ingredients

- 1 lemon, cut in half
- Here are 3 huge artichokes.
- Extra-virgin Oil, 6 tablespoonfuls
- Two peeled garlic cloves, six tablespoonfuls of dry white wine
- 3 tbsps. hashed fresh Italian parsley, divided
- 12 oz. fettuccine
- 180mL freshly grated Parmesan cheese (about 2 1/2 oz.), divided

Direction

1. A huge basin of chilly water. Put the water in a pitcher and squeeze the lemon halves into it. Put in the cut lemons. Remove the artichoke's stem one at a time. To prepare the artichoke, use the paring knife to remove the tough outer layer and slice the stem into thin rounds about 1/4 inch in diameter. You should put the stem segments in the lemon water. The artichoke leaves should be removed and thrown away. Remove the choke by spooning it out. Cut the artichoke bottoms into paper-thin slices and add them to the lemon water. To the remaining artichokes, repeat the procedure.
2. Heat the oil in a big, heavy pan over moderate heat. Sauté the garlic for a minute after adding it to the pan. Remove any excess water from the artichoke pieces and add them to the pan. To make the artichokes tender and golden, cook them for 20 minutes. Wine, please. Turn it down to low medium. Simmer the concoction, covered, for 3 minutes. Add 1 1/2 tablespoonfuls hashed parsley. Reduce heat and simmer for a minute. Throw out the garlic and add some salt and pepper to the sauce.
3. Meanwhile, seethe a pot of salted water and cook the pasta in it until it is cooked but still has a little of bite to it. Don't throw out the pasta water; instead, set aside a mug of it.

4. Drop the pasta into the cooking liquid. Toss in some artichoke sauce and half of the cheese. Toss the ingredients together, adding more of the liquid you set aside if they seem dry. Add salt and pepper to taste to the mixture. Sprinkle with the remaining cheese and 1 1/2 tablespoonfuls of parsley, then transfer to a serving dish.

43. Holly's Smoked Salmon Pasta Salad

- Serving: 4

Ingredients

- 1 (8 ounce) package farfalle (bow tie) pasta
- 30mL extra virgin Oil
- 1/2-pound cucumber, sliced
- 8 ounces smoked salmon, hashed
- 1 huge tomato, sliced
- 1 small red bell pepper, julienned
- salt and freshly ground black pepper to taste
- 125mL shredded Monterey Jack cheese, divided
- 125mL fat free blue cheese salad dressing

Direction

1. Bring a big saucepan of lightly salted water to a seethe. Cook the farfalle for 8-10 minutes, or until it reaches an al dente consistency. Drain well and then wash with cold water.
2. Toss with the Oil in a serving basin until everything is well covered. Cover and place in the refrigerator for at least 30 minutes.
3. Arrange slices of cucumber around the rims of the pasta. Sprinkle some smoked salmon, red bell pepper, and tomato on top. Season your food with pepper and salt. Dressing and Monterey Jack cheese should be added to the salad before serving.

- Serving: 10

Ingredients

- 16 ounces linguine pasta
- One-half pound of freshly sliced mushrooms
- 12 cherry tomatoes, halved
- 1 onion, hashed
- 1/2 green pepper, hashed
- roasted red peppers, one jar (four ounces), drained and hashed
- 1 cucumber, hashed
- Dressing:
- 125 ml of refined sugar
- White vinegar, 80mL
- 60mL ketchup
- 15mLonion powder
- 1 1/5mL celery seed
- 1 1/5mL Worcestershire sauce
- 1 1/5mL salt
- 1 teaspoonful ground mustard
- 1 teaspoonful paprika
- 1 teaspoonful garlic powder
- 160mL vegetable oil

Direction

1. Get a huge saucepan of lightly salted water to seething. For al dente, but still somewhat firm, linguine, seethe it for 11 minutes. Drain after rinsing with cold water.
2. Toss linguine with hashed cucumber, onion, bell peppers, cherry tomatoes, mushrooms, and red and green peppers.
3. Make a sauce by blending together garlic powder, paprika, ground mustard, salt, Worcestershire sauce, celery seed, onion powder, ketchup, vinegar, and sugar. Vegetable oil should be added to a blender in a continuous stream while the

mixture is being blended. For a few seconds, whisk until the salad dressing is thick and creamy.

4. Toss the pasta mixture with the dressing until it is evenly covered. Wrap in plastic and chill in the fridge for at least an hour.

45. Patchwork Quilt Pasta Salad

- Serving: 12

Ingredients

- Rotini or corkscrew pasta, one 12-ounce bag
- Thawed frozen mixed veggies from one 16-ounce package
- 1 (15.25 oz.) can drained kidney beans
- 375mL finely hashed celery
- 1 cucumber - peeled, seeded and hashed
- 125mL finely hashed green bell pepper
- 125mL finely hashed onion
- 160mL cider vinegar
- 30mL margarine
- 160mL sugar
- 15mLall-purpose flour
- 1/2 teaspoonful salt
- 15mLprepared brown mustard

Direction

1. Combine onion, green pepper, cucumber, celery, kidney beans, mixed vegetables, and cooked pasta in a huge bowl.
2. Brown mustard, salt, flour, sugar, margarine, and vinegar are seethed together in a skillet over moderate heat to make the dressing. For the next 5 minutes, keep cooking and stirring often. I totally dig it.
3. Toss cooled dressing with veggies in a bowl. Whisk together to disperse the dressing evenly. Refrigerate after tightly covering.

- Serving: 6

Ingredients

- 1 (8 ounce) package quinoa shells pasta
- 180mL light creamy salad dressing (such as Miracle Whip Light®)
- 180mL bacon ranch dressing
- 1-pint shredded lettuce
- 1 huge tomato, seeded and hashed
- 1 cucumber, seeded and hashed
- 3 green onions, trimmed and hashed
- 1 (3 ounce) can real bacon bits

Direction

1. Fill a big saucepan with lightly salted water and bring to a seethe. Seethe while adding the shells. Pasta should be cooked al dente in approximately 6 minutes without a lid, stirring occasionally. Please drain. Transfer to a basin and chill in the refrigerator for approximately 20 minutes.
2. In a huge bowl, incorporate bacon ranch dressing with creamy salad dressing. Stir in bacon bits, green onions, cucumber, tomato, lettuce and cooled pasta. Leave in the fridge till serving.

47. Rainbow Pasta Salad II

- Serving: 8

Ingredients

- 1 tri-colored pasta variety (16 oz.) package
- 2 big sliced tomatoes
- 1 red onion, coarsely hashed 1 cucumber, peeled and hashed
- Salad dressing of Italian origin, one 16-ounce bottle1 tri-colored pasta variety (16 oz.) package

- 2 big sliced tomatoes
- 1 red onion, coarsely hashed 1 cucumber, peeled and hashed
- Salad dressing of Italian origin, one 16-ounce bottle

Direction

1. Bring a big saucepan of lightly salted water to a seethe. The pasta should be added and cooked for 8-10 minutes, until it is cooked through but still has some bite to it. Drain and flush with cold water.
2. Toss the chilled spaghetti with the onion, cucumber, and tomatoes. Put in the fridge and chill for at least an hour, preferably more.

48. Salmon Cucumber Couscous Salad

- Serving: 4

Ingredients

- 1-pint water
- Whole wheat couscous, 1/2 a pint
- 1 boneless, skinless salmon fillet, drained and flakes from a 6-ounce can
- Cucumber (one big), celery (two stalks), tomato (one large), dried dill weed (one teaspoon)
- a pinch of freshly hashed parsley and salt to taste
- freshly ground black pepper to taste
- 15mLlemon poppy seed dressing
- 45mL extra-virgin Oil, or to taste
- 15mLdistilled white vinegar, or to taste

Direction

1. Put a pot of water over high heat so that it seethes. Toss in some couscous and turn off the heat. Leave the covered pan on the stove for 3-5 minutes. Use the fork to fluff it up. Put the couscous in a colander in the sink and run cold water over it to clean it. When cool, transfer the couscous to a serving dish. Incorporate in the dill, dill weed, parsley, cucumber, celery, salmon, tomato, salt, and pepper.

2. Incorporate the Oil, lemon poppy seed dressing, and vinegar in a small bowl. Dress the salad and serve. Be sure to give the salad a good toss so that everything is evenly distributed.

49. Colorful Bow Tie Pasta

Serving: 8

Ingredients

- Boneless pork sirloin roast seasoned with peppercorns and garlic from Smithfield®, hashed into 3/4-inch chunks
- 5 mL of garlic mince
- Fresh broccoli, hashed, 500 mL; carrots, cut, 375 mL;
- 1 mug and 60 milliliters of milk
- 30mL margarine
- 1/4 teaspoonful black pepper
- 1/4 teaspoonful Italian seasoning
- 125mL shredded mozzarella cheese
- 60mL freshly grated Parmesan cheese
- 1 huge tomato, hashed
- 2 green onions, finely hashed
- 12 ounces bow tie pasta, cooked

Direction

1. Spray a huge pan with nonstick cooking spray and heat it over high heat. Brown meat in a garlicky sauté pan. Prepare the carrots and broccoli by sautéing them until they reach a tender-crisp consistency.
2. While that's going on, combine the Italian seasoning, pepper, margarine, and milk in a small saucepan and bring to a seethe over moderate heat, stirring constantly. Turn off the fire and stir in the mozzarella and Parmesan until combined.
3. Combine cooked pasta, tomatoes, and green onions with the pork mixture. incorporate with some cheese sauce just before serving.

Serving: 8

Ingredients

- Four cups of hashed ham 375 milliliters of uncooked tri-color spiral spaghetti
- Broccoli flower buds, 375 mL
- Hashed Onion, Red, 125mL
- White Sugar, One-Third Cup
- 45 mL of mustard sauce
- 10mL salt
- 1 60mLs vegetable oil
- 80mL distilled white vinegar
- 1/2 pint halved cherry tomatoes

Direction

1. Combine the sugar, salt, and mustard in a small basin and whisk until smooth. Slowly drizzle in the oil while whisking. Put aside as you slowly whisk in the vinegar.
2. Prepare the pasta according to the directions on the box. Rinse it well with cold water, then drain it again. Enter the big basin here.
3. Combine the spaghetti with the onion, ham, and broccoli. Gently toss with the dressing until everything is uniformly coated. Cover and chill for a minimum of 2 hours. Garnish with tomatoes.

51. Lunchbox Broccoli and Ham Salad

Serving: 2

Ingredients

- 1 pouch Barilla® Ready Pasta Cut Macaroni
- 30 milliliters of pure Oil

- As desired with salt & pepper
- Juice from one lemon
- 375mL cherry tomatoes, halved
- 375mL broccoli florets, cut into small pieces
- 125mL sharp Cheddar cheese, shredded
- 1/2-pint cooked ham, julienned
- 2 hard-seethed eggs, hashed

Direction

1. Rip corner of Ready Pasta pouch to vent. Place in the microwave to heat for 1 minute; put on a plate and allow to cool down.
2. Combine lemon juice, pepper, salt and Oil and split into plastic-to-go containers.
3. To each container, put even amounts of remaining ingredients, as well as pasta, eggs, ham, cheddar cheese, broccoli, and tomatoes. Combine together with Oil-lemon juice mixture and have fun!

52. Picnic Pasta Salad

Serving: 12

Ingredients

- 1 lb. of shell-shaped pasta
- 1/4 mug hashed onions
- Cucumber, about 1/2 mug hashed
- 1/4 mug hashed cauliflower
- White Sugar, Half a Pint
- Vegetable Oil, 180 mL
- Prepared Mustard Volume: 60mL
- Mayonnaise, thirty milliliters
- White vinegar (60mL) crushed ginger (60mL) Cheddar cheese with a pinch of salt
- to taste, ground black pepper

Direction

1. Pasta should be cooked till al dente in a big saucepan of seething salted water. Scrub in lukewarm water. Do not clog the drains.
2. Meanwhile, toss hashed veggies with a mixture of vinegar, mayonnaise, mustard, oil, sugar, and grated Cheddar cheese in a huge bowl. Season with pepper and salt, to taste. The two should be combined well. Incorporate spaghetti. Put in the fridge for at least 2 hours and up to 4 hours before serving.

53. The Ultimate Pasta Salad

Serving: 12

Ingredients

- 1 uncooked packet of tri-colored spiral pasta (about 16 ounces)
- 1 head fresh broccoli, cut into bite size pieces
- One fresh head of cauliflower, broken up into manageable chunks
- 1 red onion, hashed
- 5mL minced garlic
- 8 ounces pepperoni slices, cut into quarters
- Cubed mozzarella cheese from 1 (8-ounce) box
- Huge black olives from a can, drained and sliced (1 can, 6 ounces total)
- 125mL Oil, or to taste
- 125mL red wine vinegar, or to taste
- to taste with salt and pepper
- To taste, Italian seasoning

Direction

1. Bring a big saucepan of water to a seethe and gently salt it. Pasta should be cooked in salted water until al dente, about 8-10 minutes. Transfer to a covered basin and refrigerate for at least an hour, preferably longer.
2. Toss together cold spaghetti, red wine vinegar, Oil, olives, pepperoni, mozzarella, garlic, red onion, cauliflower, and broccoli. Season with pepper, salt, and Italian seasoning. Put in the fridge and wait to serve cold.

Serving: 16

Ingredients

- rotini pasta, whole wheat (one 16-ounce bag)
- 1 ½ pints hashed broccoli
- 1-pint cubed cucumber
- 375mL cubed butternut squash
- 375mL halved green beans
- 375mL cubed jicama
- 1/2-pint Italian dressing, or more to taste
- 125mL halved snow peas
- 1/2 head cauliflower, hashed
- 30mL halved cherry tomatoes

Direction

1. Bring around four quarts of water to a seethe with a pinch of salt. Substitute pasta. Keep stirring for the next 7 minutes, or until the vegetables are tender. Pasta should be drained in a colander and then rinsed in cold water.
2. Combine spaghetti with cherry tomatoes, cauliflower, snow peas, jicama, green beans, squash, cucumber, broccoli, and Italian dressing. Put in the refrigerator until cooled.

55. Rutabaga Salad

- Serving: 6

Ingredients

- 1 rutabaga, peeled and cut into 1/4-inch chunks
- 1-pint water
- 15mLvegetable oil
- 375mL couscous

- 125mL nutritional yeast
- 60mL vegetable oil
- 60mL apple cider vinegar
- 1 1/5mL honey
- 1 teaspoonful Italian seasoning
- 1 teaspoonful dried oregano
- 1 teaspoonful dried dill weed
- 1/2 teaspoonful ground black pepper
- 1/4 teaspoonful cayenne pepper
- 1 pinch salt to taste (optional)

Direction

1. In a saucepan, put a steamer insert. Fill water to just below the steamer's bottom; seethe. Add rutabaga. Steam for 10 minutes until just tender.
2. Bring 1 tablespoonful of vegetable oil and 1 pint of water to a seethe in a sauce pan. turn down the stove. Toss the couscous in. Cover. Wait 14 minutes to see whether the water has been absorbed. Toss with a fork to fluff.
3. In a big bowl, incorporate cayenne pepper, black pepper, dill, oregano, Italian seasoning, honey, apple cider vinegar, 60mL vegetable oil and nutritional yeast.
4. Incorporate rutabaga and couscous into the nutritional yeast dressing. Season using salt.

56. Caribbean Crabmeat Salad

- Serving: 4

Ingredients

- 1 ½ pints uncooked rotini pasta
- 1 (8 ounce) package imitation crabmeat, flaked
- 1 red bell pepper, julienned
- 1 mango - peeled, seeded, and cubed
- 30mL hashed fresh cilantro
- 1 jalapeno pepper, seeded and minced
- 1 teaspoonful lime zest
- 45mL fresh lime juice

- 30mL Oil
- 15mLhoney
- 1/2 teaspoonful ground cumin
- 1/2 teaspoonful ground ginger
- 1/4 teaspoonful salt

Direction

1. Seethe a big pot with lightly salted water. Put pasta. Cook till al dente for 8-10 minutes. Drain. Use cold water to rinse.
2. In a big bowl, put jalapeno, cilantro, mango, red pepper, crabmeat and pasta. Put aside.
3. Whisk salt, ginger, cumin, honey, Oil, lime juice and lime zest in a small bowl. Put on salad. Toss till coated. In the fridge, let sit for an hour minimum before serving.

57. Home Town Drive in Pasta Salad

- Serving: 8

Ingredients

- White sugar, 60 mL 1 box (12 ounces) of tri-colored rotini pasta
- 1 teaspoonful salt
- 30mL hot water
- 60mL white vinegar
- 30mL vegetable oil
- 15mLdried oregano
- 1 huge tomato, hashed
- 1 red bell pepper, hashed
- 60mL finely hashed sweet onion
- 1 (8 ounce) package shredded sharp Cheddar cheese
- 1 pinch ground black pepper to taste (optional)

Direction

1. Cook rotini pasta in a huge pot of gently salted seething water for 8 minutes, or

until al dente, then drain and refresh under cold running water.

2. In a very huge salad bowl, combine the seething water, salt, and sugar and stir until there are no more sugar lumps. Dressing: combine oregano, vegetable oil, vinegar, and sugar. Throw in some hashed tomato, red bell pepper, and onion. Combine the rotini, veggies, and dressing in a huge bowl, and gently toss in the cheese and pepper.

58. Springtime Pasta Salad

- Serving: 8

Ingredients

- Tiny Veggie Spiral Pasta, 1 Ounce
- One cuke, prepped by peeling, seeding, and chopping
- 125 ml of black olives, sliced
- 60 ml of red onion, hashed
- 125mL mayonnaise
- 60mL sour cream
- 1 1/4 teaspoonfuls dill weed
- 1/2 teaspoonful salt
- 1/2 teaspoonful dry mustard
- 1/4 teaspoonful garlic salt

Direction

1. Get a huge saucepan of lightly salted water to seething. Pasta should be seethed for 8 minutes until it is cooked but still has some bite to it. Drain. Pasta should be cooled by rinsing it in cold water. Drain. Create a huge basin for the pasta.
2. In a bowl, incorporate garlic salt, dry mustard, salt, dill, sour cream, mayonnaise, red onion, black olives and cucumber. Put on paste. Evenly coat by gently mixing/
3. Use plastic wrap to cover the bowl. Keep in fridge for 2 hours prior to serving.

- Serving: 4

Ingredients

- Macaroni, one pint
- 1 grated carrot 1 sliced green bell pepper 1 tiny onion
- 60mL mayonnaise
- 60mL Ranch-style salad dressing

Direction

1. In a huge saucepan, bring a few tablespoonfuls of salt to a seethe. Pasta should be cooked for 8-10 minutes, until it reaches the al dente stage; then drained. Scrub with cold water and put in a huge dish.
2. Incorporate the spaghetti with the vegetables (carrot, pepper, and onion). Toss in with ranch dressing and some mayonnaise. Adjust the dressing and mayonnaise to your preference and serve.

60. Eagle Salad

- Serving: 5

Ingredients

- 1-pint elbow macaroni
- 45mL mayonnaise
- One five-ounce can of tuna, drained, hashed half an onion, salt and freshly ground black pepper to taste

Direction

1. Bring a big saucepan of lightly salted water to a seethe. Add the macaroni and simmer for 8 minutes, or until al dente but still somewhat firm to the bite. Rinse it down the drain with cold water to cool it down. Put away to dry for a while.

2. Incorporate the chilled macaroni with the tuna, onion, and mayonnaise in a bowl. You may add additional mayonnaise if you like the flavor. Season with salt and black pepper. Until ready to serve, store in the fridge.

61. Elbow Macaroni and Kidney Bean Salad

- Serving: 8

Ingredients

- One-half mug of elbow macaroni
- Red kidney beans from one 15-ounce can, drained and rinsed
- About 125 milliliters of hashed celery
- Light Mayonnaise, 125 ml
- 60mL hashed onion
- 30mL red wine vinegar, or to taste
- salt and ground black pepper to taste

Direction

1. Put the water in the big saucepan and bring it to a seethe with the mild salt. In a pot of seething water, cook elbow macaroni for 6-8 minutes, stirring periodically. Maintain a little bite of firmness during cooking. Cold water straining and rinsing.
2. Combine the cooked macaroni, celery, kidney beans, red wine vinegar, onion, light mayonnaise, black pepper, salt, and red wine vinegar in a dish. Put in the fridge and let cool for at least two hours.

62. Hawaiiani Bruddah Potato Mac (Maccaroni) Salad

- Serving: 20

Ingredients

- 5 eggs
- 7 huge potatoes, peeled and cubed
- 1/2-pint elbow macaroni

- 1 ½ pints mayonnaise
- 15mLsherry vinegar (optional)
- 1 1/5mL curry powder
- 1 teaspoonful celery seed
- black pepper and salt to taste
- Carrots, grated, one pint
- Green peas, 1/2 pint frozen, seethed and drained
- 1 tiny, hashed sweet onion

Direction

1. Put the eggs in a single layer in a saucepan and cover them with water by an inch. In order to get a rolling seethe, you must first cover the pot and turn the heat up high. When the water comes to a seethe, turn off the heat and let the eggs sit in the water for 15 minutes. To chill eggs, drain the hot water and replace it with cold running water in the sink. Peel and slice the eggs after they have cooled down.
2. Bring a big saucepan of salted water to a seethe. Add potatoes and simmer for 15 minutes, or until cooked but still somewhat firm. Drain and chill in the fridge.
3. Bring a big saucepan of water to a rapid seethe with a pinch of salt over high heat. After the water has returned to a seethe, add the macaroni and toss to combine. Turn the heat up to high, remove the lid, and seethe the pasta for 8 minutes, turning regularly, until it is al dente but still has some bite. Colanders may be used to drain pasta in the sink. Rinse with cold water.
4. Incorporate the pepper, salt, celery seed, curry powder, vinegar, and mayonnaise together in a bowl. Incorporate the cooled potatoes, macaroni, hashed eggs, onion, peas, and carrots in a huge bowl. Add the dressing cautiously and incorporate well. Cover and refrigerate overnight for best results.

Dessert Recipes

63. Honey Mustard Macaroni Salad

- Serving: 12

Ingredients

- 1 package of elbow macaroni (16 ounces)
- 6 sliced hard-seethed eggs
- 125mL hashed onion
- 125mL hashed celery
- 125mL hashed green bell pepper
- 1-pint mayonnaise
- 1/2-pint milk
- 125mL sweet pickle relish
- 80mL prepared honey mustard
- 1/2 teaspoonful sea salt
- 1/4 teaspoonful ground black pepper

Direction

1. Get a huge saucepan of water to a seethe and season it gently with salt. Cook the elbow macaroni in a pot of seething water, stirring periodically, for 8 minutes, or until al dente. Macaroni should be cooled by being drained and washed under cold water. Add the macaroni to the salad in the huge bowl.
2. Then add hard-cooked eggs, green bell pepper, celery, and onion to the pasta and stir. Toss the salad with the dressing, which was prepared by combining honey mustard, pickle relish, milk, and mayonnaise, then seasoning to taste with ground black pepper and sea salt.

64. Macaroni Salad

- Serving: 75

Ingredients

- Macaroni, ten pounds
- Twelve eggs 45 milliliters of vegetable oil salt six hashed onions three hashed green bell peppers two hashed carrots
- 1/2-pound cooked ham, hashed
- 3 cloves garlic, crushed
- 1/2-pint Oil
- 1-pint mayonnaise
- 45mL balsamic vinegar
- salt and pepper to taste

Direction

1. Bring a huge amount of water and a pinch of salt to a seethe. Cook the macaroni in a pot of salted seething water for 30 minutes, or until it reaches the desired texture (al dente), then remove from the heat and drain.
2. Put the eggs in a huge saucepan and cover them with cold water. Bring to a seethe over moderate heat. Simmer the eggs for 12-17 minutes at a low heat. Remove the pan from the stove immediately and cool it down by rinsing it with cold water. The eggs should be removed from the water, peeled, and then cut into little pieces.

3. Incorporate the hashed eggs, ham, onion, and carrots with the hashed bell pepper in a huge bowl. Oil, balsamic vinegar, garlic, pepper, mayonnaise, and salt should be mixed together in a separate bowl.
4. Combine the macaroni that has been cooked, the egg mixture, and the mayonnaise mixture in a huge bowl.

65. Macaroni And Cheese Salad

- Serving: 6

Ingredients

- 375mL macaroni
- 30mL cider vinegar
- 1/2-pint shredded Cheddar cheese
- 125mL hashed green bell pepper
- 60mL hashed celery
- 45mL thinly sliced green onion
- 8 cherry tomatoes
- 1/2-pint mayonnaise
- salt and pepper to taste
- 1/4 teaspoonful Beau Monde ™ seasoning

Direction

1. Prepare pasta according to package directions, then drain and rinse under cool water.
2. Combine the pasta and vinegar in a huge basin. Give it a good stir, then set it aside for 15 to 20 minutes.
3. Add in seasonings, mayonnaise, tomatoes, green onions, celery, peppers and cheese. Stir them well and keep it chilled in the refrigerator.

- Serving: 16

Ingredients

- 16 ounces uncooked elbow macaroni
- 4 carrots, shredded
- 1 huge red onion, hashed
- 1/2 green bell pepper, seeded and hashed
- 1/2 red bell pepper, seeded and hashed
- 1/2-pint hashed celery
- 1-pint mayonnaise
- 1 (14 ounce) can sweetened condensed milk
- 125mL white sugar
- 125mL white vinegar
- salt and pepper to taste

Direction

1. Slightly salt a huge saucepan of water and bring it to a seethe. Macaroni should be added and cooked for 8 minutes or until tender. Use cold water and then squeeze out the water.
2. Put the celery, peppers, onions, and carrots in a huge basin. incorporate in the condensed milk, mayonnaise, sugar, pepper, salt, vinegar, and sugar. Toss the macaroni gently with the sauce, cover, and chill for at least 8 hours. You can prepare this a day ahead of time, and the flavors will blend as long as you stir it every so often. Some of the liquid will be absorbed by the macaroni.

67. Mushroom Mint Pasta Salad

- Serving: 12

Ingredients

- Farfalle (bow tie) pasta, one 16-ounce box

- 60mL Oil, divided
- 2 (8 ounce) packages button mushrooms, sliced
- 4 onions, sliced
- 10 sprigs fresh mint
- 15mL white sugar
- 1 pinch salt
- 1 pinch ground black pepper

Direction

1. Lightly salt the water and bring it to a seethe in a big saucepan. Cook the pasta until it reaches the desired texture (al dente), usually between 8 and 10 minutes. Once cooled, transfer to a serving dish. Oil (around 45 mL) should be combined.
2. The remaining Oil should be heated over moderate heat in a big pan. Onions and mushrooms should be added to the pan. Keep stirring it as it cooks to ensure even browning. Slowly pour in the heavy cream while swirling constantly. Place mint leaves in pan. Stir constantly for 5 minutes to cook.
3. Cream sauce needs sugar, so stir some in. Season with salt and pepper. You may get rid of the mint leaves by using a slotted spoon. Coat the spaghetti with the sauce and stir it in.

68. Asian Rice Noodle Salad

- Serving: 8

Ingredients

- Reduced-sodium soy sauce, 80mL
- Seasoned rice wine vinegar, one-third cup
- 60mL lime juice
- 30mL chili paste with garlic
- 15mLsesame oil
- 15mLminced fresh ginger root
- 1 teaspoonful dried mint
- Noodles, rice, 8 ounces
- 1 lb. of lean pork ground
- ½-pint thinly sliced green onions

- ½-pint hashed cilantro
- ½-pint thinly sliced snow peas
- 1 huge red onion, quartered and thinly sliced
- 60mL roasted peanuts

Direction

1. In a tight-fitting lidded jar, incorporate mint, ginger root, sesame oil, chili paste with garlic, lime juice, rice wine vinegar and soy sauce; keep it covered and shake till the sauce is blended well.
2. Seethe a big water pot; put in noodles and cook for roughly 5 minutes till soft. Drain, cool down, and add into a serving bowl. Use kitchen shears to chop noodles.
3. Heat a huge skillet over moderate heat. For a browned and crumbly pork, cook and toss it in a hot pan for about 7 minutes, then drain, discard the fat, and cool it on paper towels. Fill noodle bowls with meat.
4. Combine red onion, snow peas, cilantro and green onions with noodles and pork.
5. Add peanuts into a heavy bag that is resealable; seal and crush a bit using a big glass or the jar bottom. Put peanuts into the noodle mixture. Pour in sauce and incorporate well.

69. Chinese Cold Pasta Salad

- Serving: 4

Ingredients

- 8 ounces dry fettuccine pasta
- 30mL natural peanut butter
- 125mL vegetable broth
- 30mL soy sauce
- 3 cloves garlic, minced
- 5mL crushed red pepper flakes
- 1 red bell pepper, hashed
- 2 green onions, hashed
- 125mL hashed fresh cilantro

Direction

1. Pour water in a big pot and bring it to a seethe, put pasta in and cook until al dente. Rinse and strain. Put aside.
2. Incorporate crushed red pepper, garlic, soy sauce, broth, and peanut butter in a big bowl. Incorporate thoroughly. Add in pasta, cilantro, scallions, and sliced red pepper and incorporate to combine. Let chill.

70. Wild Mushroom and Spinach Pasta

- Serving Size: 4

Ingredients:

- 2 large chopped shallots
- 2 tbsp. olive oil
- 3 cups chestnut mushrooms, finely diced
- 2 thyme leaves
- 2 tbsp. butter
- ⅔ cup heavy cream
- 2 cloves garlic
- 1 cup fresh parmesan cheese
- 1 ½ baby spinach, chopped
- 4 cups pine nuts, roasted
- 7 oz. linguine
- ½ tbsp. black pepper
- 2 tbsp. salt
- 2 long parsley leaves for garnishing

Directions:

1. Put one tablespoon of salt, one-half tablespoon of olive oil, and water into a big saucepan.
2. The water should be brought to a boil over a high to medium burner, and then two cups of pasta should be added.
3. Begin boiling the pasta according to the instructions provided on the pasta

package.

4. In a separate sauté pan, add the oil and shallots, and then saute them over medium heat for ten minutes, or until the shallots have become tender.
5. Put the butter in the frying pan. The mushrooms should then be cooked correctly. Continue cooking until the mushroom releases its juices.
6. Cook for a further 5 minutes after adding the garlic and thyme leaves, then season with salt and black pepper.
7. Pour the cream into the bowl, and then stir in three tablespoons of the reserved pasta water. Make sure you stir it well.
8. After adding the cheese and stirring for five minutes, set the oven to broil. When the cheese is added, the melting process causes the heat to be turned off.
9. After that, stir in the spinach. Give the ingredients a good toss.
10. After adding the boiled pasta, stir the mixture for a further two minutes.
11. After the pasta has been combined with the sauce, add pine nuts to the dish.
12. Garnish with some finely chopped fresh parsley.

Conclusion

The delightful culinary adventure that we have set out on within the pages of "Pasta Cookbook Homemade" has taken us through both time and space as we have investigated the history of pasta, mastered the essential equipment for making pasta, perfected the art of cooking pasta, and discovered the numerous sauces and pairings that turn simple ingredients into memorable meals. Let's pause for a second to think back on the diverse array of tastes, sensations, and customs that we've experienced on our journey with pasta, as well as the gastronomic knowledge that we've picked up along the way.

Throughout the whole of this book, the overarching theme has been very clear: pasta is a blank canvas on which we may freely express our culinary aspirations. We have fashioned a universe of flavor experiences from the most basic of components, which include flour, water, and a pinch of salt. These creations range from cozy classics to daring originals. Pasta is a dish that has woven its way through many different cultures and countries, as well as time and space, to become a global icon that represents coziness, festivity, and coming together with others.

Pasta's roots may be traced all the way back to the Etruscans and Greeks, all the way to the furthest reaches of the Silk Road, and all the way to the busy kitchens of Italian immigrants in America. This information has been unearthed by us. This intricately woven history of pasta serves as a reminder that culinary customs are a living testimony to the inventiveness and versatility of the human race, and have done so for ages by bringing people together around the table.

After reading about the many instruments that are necessary for making pasta, you should now have everything you need to make pasta that is up to your standards in your own home kitchen. You've discovered that creating pasta is not an arcane skill but rather an approachable craft that anybody can perfect with the correct direction and a dash of love. This realization applies to both the reliable pasta machine and the straightforward rolling pin.

In the course of our search for the ideal pasta, we uncovered the techniques that enable al dente pasta to be cooked to a texture that is both soft and firm in every bite. This achievement is a demonstration of our commitment to achieving the highest possible standards in the culinary arts. You now have the knowledge and skills necessary to achieve pasta nirvana in your own house, which will enable you to appreciate the actual essence of this well-loved meal. This will be possible since you have gained these advantages.

You have discovered, as we have gone through a symphony of sauces and taste combinations, that pasta is a flexible chameleon that is capable of adjusting to a kaleidoscope of different flavors. You've learned that the right combination can take an ordinary pasta dish and turn it into something extraordinary, from the reassuring embrace of tomato sauces to the luxurious caress of creations based on cream. This is because the right pairing can elevate a pasta dish from the ordinary to the extraordinary. This beautiful waltz of pasta and sauce is a demonstration of the many opportunities for artistic expression that are waiting for you in the kitchen.

Have we been able to keep the promise that we made? Have we given you the resources, the information, and the motivation to become a pasta master in your own right? The solution is waiting for you in the form of exciting new gastronomic experiences. The quality of our work can be judged not only by the words that appear on these pages, but also by the aromas that waft from your kitchen, the laughter and conversation that can be heard around your dinner table, and the happiness that can be brought to your loved ones by a pasta dish that has been expertly crafted.

As you get to the end of "Pasta Cookbook Homemade," there is one thing I want you to take away with you, and that is the conviction that when it comes to pasta, your creative potential is unbounded. Remember that every meal is a chance to exhibit your culinary expertise, whether you are making a basic midweek dinner or a feast for a special event. Whether you are constructing a simple weeknight supper or cooking a feast for a special occasion, every meal is an opportunity.

But beyond the artistry and the tastes, pasta is a symbol of connection and community. Pasta is the food that brings people together. It is a dish that unites people, across national boundaries and linguistic barriers, and encourages us to take joy in the simple pleasures that life has to offer. It serves as a good reminder that the act of eating a meal with other people, whether they family or friends, is a celebration of love, togetherness, and the happiness that comes from just being alive.

Therefore, when you embark on your very own pasta-making adventures, equipped with the information and ideas provided in this book, I urge you to approach the kitchen with a feeling of surprise and curiosity. Accept the flaws, relish the triumphs, and most importantly, treat the people you care about to your culinary works of art.

In conclusion, "Pasta Cookbook Homemade" is more than simply a cookbook; rather, it is an open invitation to go on a voyage of culinary discovery and creation that will last a lifetime. It is a celebration of the enduring fascination of pasta as well as the delight that comes from preparing memorable meals with loved ones and sharing them with them. As you gain more self-assurance and go back into the kitchen, I pray that the pasta meals you create will be a shining example of the alchemy that occurs when one's passion and heritage are brought together in a recipe. Have a good meal, and may your experiences with pasta be as varied and exciting as your imagination allows for them to be!

Made in United States
Troutdale, OR
04/30/2024

19488705R10051